AFX
5828

W9-CAP-371

KARSH

KARSH

❖ **AMERICAN LEGENDS** ❖

Photographs and Commentary by Yousuf Karsh

BULFINCH PRESS

LITTLE, BROWN AND COMPANY

BOSTON · TORONTO · LONDON

First Edition

Springs of Achievement Series on the Art of Photography

Library of Congress Cataloging-in-Publication Data

Karsh, Yousuf.
  Karsh, American legends : photographs and commentary / by Yousuf Karsh. — 1st ed.
    160 p. 24.3 x 30.6 cm.
  "A Bulfinch Press book."
  Includes index.
  ISBN 0-8212-1906-5
  1. Celebrities—United States—Portraits. I. Title. II. Title: American legends.
TR681.F3K3742 1992
779'.2'092—dc20   *92–8508*

Bulfinch Press is an imprint and trademark of Little, Brown and Company (Inc.)

Published simultaneously in Canada by Little, Brown & Company (Canada) Limited

Frontispiece: Yousuf Karsh, by George O'Neill, Jr.

PRINTED IN SWITZERLAND

To my wife, Estrellita,
who conceived the idea for this book,

and to the memory of our dear friend
John Maclaurin,
who nurtured it

Angela Lansbury, 1946, at the beginning of her career

❖ INTRODUCTION ❖

During my photographic odyssey spanning more than half a century, my life has been enriched by many remarkable men and women, who have inspired me with their artistry and dedication. When my portrait of Winston Churchill was published in 1941, it marked the beginning of my worldwide travels and my encounters with those fascinating personalities who have shaped our era.

The photographs in this book have been taken close to home. The creative publisher Jeffrey Butler invited me to photograph Helen Hayes at her Nyack, New York, retreat for *VISàVIS,* the United Airlines magazine, and this became the springboard for a subsequent series of new portraits called "American Legends."

The definition of the word "legend" has evolved from its Latin origin of "reading together" into "a story, generally of a marvelous character." And these distinguished Americans, who had woven their own lives into a story of marvellous character, it would now be my challenging task to portray.

Unlike my other books, for this American collection I did not have the luxury of choosing my subjects from portraits I had taken over a long period of time. For two intensive years, ending in 1991, I photographed most of these men and women whose gifts – intellectual, artistic, spiritual – are continuing to enrich our national life.

Some of them are household words, people with whom many of us grew up and who are part of our shared memory. Others, acknowledged as supreme masters in their own fields, have only recently been propelled into the public consciousness.

Each has made a unique contribution to the spirit of America.

Wherever possible, I tried to photograph each "legend" in his or her own environment. My travels took me all over America, from the sophisticated opulence of Helen Gurley Brown's New York apartment to the simple wooden building, thunderbird symbols framing the doorway, of Cesar Chavez's labor union headquarters in rural California; from collector Walter Annenberg's Pennsylvania estate with exquisite Impressionist paintings on its walls, to Mother Hale's modest rooms in Harlem, decorated with Mickey Mouse cutouts and her "children's" mittens. These journeys only emphasized anew the diversity in this great land, where excellence exists everywhere.

One of the unexpected gratifications of preparing *American Legends* has been the opportunity to meet once again and renew my friendship with people I first photographed several decades ago, early in their careers. These "second time around" reunions were especially heartwarming. The years had only enhanced their personal and artistic development and fine-honed their craft. An informal and confident Angela Lansbury showed me the superb roses she cultivated in her home garden – a great contrast to the shy, wide-eyed, diffident eighteen-year-old actress I first met. She told me she remembered every detail of our first session.

Julie Harris, as Joan of Arc in Jean Anouilh's play The Lark, *1956*

Charlton Heston and his son, Fraser, at home, 1956

With Julie Harris, I have maintained a cordial friendship since I portrayed her as a young "Joan of Arc." She came before my lens again, wearing magical ancient African amber beads, in the fullness of her maturity as an artist.

During the filming of Cecil B. De Mille's *Ten Commandments* in Hollywood, I first met that great actor and gentleman, Charlton Heston. While visiting at his home, I took an impromptu photograph of him holding his then two-year-old son, Fraser; they were just out of the shower, draped in fresh towels. Thirty-six years later, Charlton and Lydia Heston, searching for a unique memento for Fraser, recalled the photograph and asked me to prepare it for him as their Christmas gift. It came as a tender surprise for Fraser, who had never seen it before.

I must confess that as an inveterate dog lover, I am always delighted when anticipatory barks follow the ringing of the doorbell, for I know that in addition to an eminent master or mistress, I will meet a much-loved pet. I have fond memories of our own American citizen, our French poodle, Clicquot. The image of the great basketball star Bob Cousy cradling in his arms an animated ball of white fluff, his toy poodle Rebecca, remains with me as a poignant vignette. So strong was the bond between Bobby Short and his Dalmatian, Chili, that with the self-confidence of one who was sure of his place, Chili demanded to become part of the photograph – and did! Bear, the black Labrador retriever of General H. Norman Schwarzkopf, having been denied eight long months of his beloved master's presence during the Persian Gulf War, would not leave his side during our photographic session.

There is a photograph that will always be meaningful to me, of a carefree trio enjoying each other's company – Jim Henson, Kermit the Frog, and their ardent admirer, Yousuf Karsh. Surrounded by his talented family and colleagues, and the magical creatures into whom he breathed life, I found the creative atmosphere of Henson's workshop exhilarating. When he learned that I had photographed the great Russian puppeteer Sergei Obratzov in the early sixties, Henson presented me with tape cassettes showing him working with him and other puppet masters. No one could have foreseen Jim Henson's untimely death a short time afterward; it came as such a shocking final severance, so enthusiastically did he embrace life, and so warm and generous was his spirit. I was honored when his family requested that a selection of photographs from our sitting be placed on a special table at Jim Henson's memorial service at the Cathedral of St. John the Divine.

The personalities in this book comprise only a small sample of the extraordinary gifted people who make up the fabric of America. I hope I have given the viewer an intimate glimpse – a fresh insight – into their minds and spirits.

— Yousuf Karsh

❖ AMERICAN LEGENDS ❖

JUDITH JAMISON, *Artistic Director of Alvin Ailey American Dance Theater, Dancer*
Alvin Ailey chose her to carry on his American Dance Theater – the legacy of black American experience.
"Focus," she advises her dancers, "luxuriate; wrap yourself around the music."

JEROME ROBBINS, *Choreographer, Theater Director*

He is as unsparing of himself as of his dancers in his quest for excellence. The grace of his movements complements the grace of his spirit.

MARTHA GRAHAM, *Choreographer, Dancer*
 While I photographed her, she was sitting on a stool in a low room, but she seemed to be dancing
 as if she had the space of a great stage around her.

GEORGE ABBOTT, *Theater Producer, Director, Playwright*
    Over a century old, he retains his sharp wit, lack of pretense, and let's-get-with-it attitude. What would the American musical theater be without "Mr. Abbott"? As one writer put it: "He *is* the Broadway musical!"

STEPHEN SONDHEIM, *Composer, Lyricist*

It did not surprise me to learn that he loves intricate games and puzzles. They mirror the subtle complexity of his mind – and his inherent sense of fun.

HAROLD PRINCE, *Theater and Film Director, Producer, Writer*
The peerless producer-director had spent countless hours planning his next production, and as he enthusiastically shared his vision with me, it took shape before my eyes.

ARTHUR MILLER, *Playwright*

"Everyone has agonies. The difference is that I try to take my agonies home and teach them to sing."

— Arthur Miller

JIM HENSON, *Puppeteer, Creator of the Muppets, Television Director and Producer*
 Journalist Jonathan Schwartz mourned this "Professor of Growing Up . . . (who) swooped up our kids in
 the gentle process of discovery." It was a joy to watch the beguiling creatures of his imagination
 spring to life at his masterful touch.

LEONARD BERNSTEIN, *Composer, Conductor, Pianist*

His exquisite impromptu piano reveries – poetic islands of peace – punctuated the tension of a highly charged photographic session.

MARILYN HORNE, *Vocal Artist*

The great soprano came into my Ottawa studio unannounced on a cold winter day bearing golden oranges and the gift of her friendship. Here, she is absorbed in her own inner music.

JESSYE NORMAN, *Vocal Artist*

An awesome, gracious goddess, disciplined and devoted to her art, who delighted me with her girlish levity and infectious humor.

RUDOLF SERKIN, *Piano Virtuoso*

His daughter was amused as this gentle piano virtuoso, who supremely interpreted the classical composers, pleaded ignorance of the existence of famous "rock stars."

ISAAC STERN, *Violinist*

Everything in his formidable artistry is based on his human compassion. Making music and listening to young people keep him young. How, I asked, did he save Carnegie Hall from destruction? "By being innocent enough not to realize how difficult it was!"

PHILIP GLASS, *Composer*

In his cluttered music room he produces avant-garde compositions — beyond the parameters of conventional music — challenging us to open our minds and relinquish the comfort of familiar melodies.

DIZZY GILLESPIE, *Jazz Musician, Composer*

Although the co-inventor of bebop "changed the whole concept of American music," the trumpet was not his instrument of first choice. Luckily for the development of jazz, his arms were too short for the trombone!

DAVE BRUBECK, *Jazz Pianist, Composer*

Behind his masterly chords of incomparable jazz, I saw a religious man committed to the betterment of the world.

BOBBY SHORT, *Jazz Pianist, Singer*

The urbane musician opened a celebratory bottle of champagne while he and his Dalmatian, Chili, companionably shared the flickering candlelight. The next day they left for Paris.

GORDON PARKS, *Photographer, Film Director, Writer, Composer*

My gifted colleague did what is most difficult for a photographer – he put aside his expertise and became a collaborator on the other side of the camera.

BERENICE ABBOTT, *Photographer*

In her Maine cottage, far removed from the New York metropolis she portrayed, this direct and fiercely independent pioneer photographer shared anecdotes about our mutual friend and her mentor, Man Ray.

CORNELL CAPA, *Founder and Director of International Center of Photography,*
Photographer

His 1974 concept of a center devoted exclusively to photography
has come to fruition largely because of his persuasive dedication.
He has an uncanny ability to so involve you in his dream
that you, too, wish to become part of it.

51

R. C. GORMAN, *Artist*

His art now enjoys international popularity, but this gregarious world traveler has never abandoned his Navajo roots, his artistic inspiration, nor his deep attachment to the land and the people of New Mexico.

HELEN FRANKENTHALER, *Artist*

Of her lyrical abstract expressionist paintings, she has commented,
"Every canvas is a journey all its own." Photographing her,
we shared our own artistic journey.

JASPER JOHNS, *Artist*

In our photographic session, he was a sensitive collaborator, intuitively anticipating and
aware of all the nuances of light and shadow.

MILTON GLASER, *Graphic Designer*
   The eager young draftsmen in his studio greeted his return from a retrospective exhibition
   in Spain. His artistic decorations, murals, and posters transcend advertising and design,
   and have become part of our everyday culture.

ANDY WARHOL, *Artist*

Restless, curious, he photographed me, my assistant, the landmark mansion across the street. "I know how my paintings will look," he commented, "but photographs are always a surprise to me."

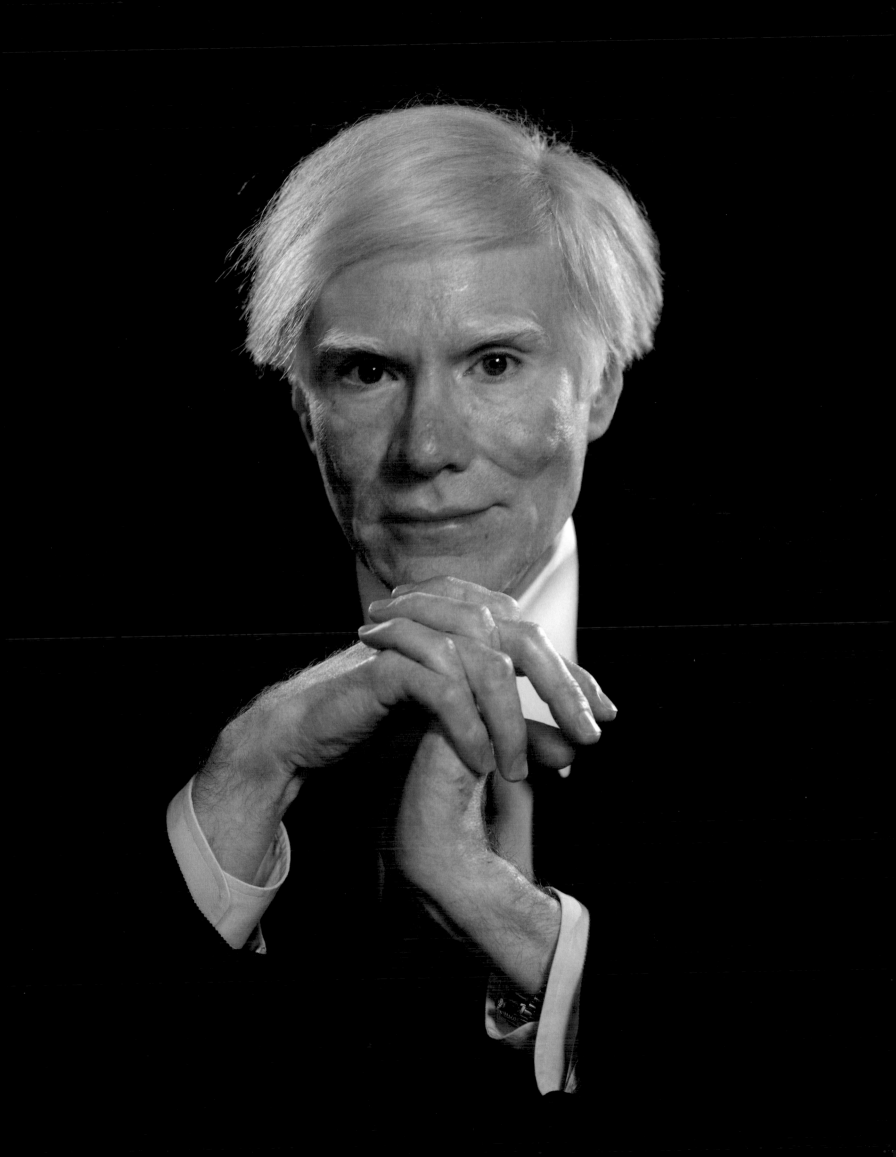

GEOFFREY BEENE, *Fashion Designer*

His easy, courtly Southern demeanor belies the intensity of his creative inner world — a unique realm where current high fashion becomes timeless art.

I. M. PEI, *Architect*

He reminisced about acquiring his first important sculpture from a supportive Jacques Lipchitz when he was just beginning his career.

PHILIP JOHNSON, *Architect*

We talked of the satisfaction it gave this eminent architect to look out his window and see his AT&T building silhouetted against the New York sky.

J. CARTER BROWN, *Former Director of National Gallery of Art*

In sharp contrast to the overflowing richness of the National Gallery, his office was a quiet, almost ascetic oasis, decorated with a few personally chosen works of art, reflecting his discriminating taste.

LEO CASTELLI, *Art Dealer*

Despite his twentieth-century Rauschenberg painting, I felt this unassuming connoisseur of contemporary art would have been equally at home as Grand Vizier in *The Arabian Nights*.

DOMINIQUE DE MENIL, *Art Collector and Patron*

There must be a spiritual link between this eminent art collector and the great patrons of the Renaissance, who combined steely determination with unerring taste.

WALTER ANNENBERG, *Philanthropist, Publisher*

He spoke of making art available to the "broad masses," and of how he and his wife personally chose and related to each painting in his magnificent Impressionist and Postimpressionist collection.

DAVID ROCKEFELLER, *Philanthropist*

With aristocratic dignity and grace, he has shouldered the formidable mantle of his family's ongoing commitment to the welfare of society, through its tradition of philanthropy.

JAMES WATSON, *Nobel Laureate (Medicine), Scientist*

The informal and charming Nobelist, not content to rest on the laurels of his spectacular, youthful discovery of the structure of DNA, is now himself an inspiring mentor to a group of brilliant young research scientists.

EDWIN LAND, *Founder of Polaroid Corporation, Physicist, Inventor*

When did Polaroid begin? The shy scientist replied, "When my son asked me why he could not immediately see the photographs after clicking the shutter."

HAROLD EDGERTON, *Professor, Inventor*

I could understand why the brilliant inventor of strobe lights was persuaded not to retire from the MIT faculty; he was such a beloved teacher and gave so much to his students.

JONAS SALK, *Physician, Scientist*
Philosopher as well as scientist, the codiscoverer of the polio vaccine now seeks "the promised land" in his search for cures for cancer and AIDS.

ISAAC ASIMOV, *Author*

The late, prolific author did not permit anyone to enter the room where he created his worlds of science fiction, so we decided that the Museum of Natural History in New York would make an appropriate alternate setting for photography.

MOTHER CLARA HALE, *Founder of Hale House, a Home for Children of Drug-addicted and AIDS Mothers*
To be with this frail, compassionate woman among her "children" is to feel her faith and power — her faith in God, and the power of love.

RALPH NADER, *Consumer Advocate, Social Reformer*

He has shown us the impact one man can make on society. The public image of the consumer
activist is stern, serious, and dedicated. I found also a man of self-deprecating humor and warmth.

CESAR CHAVEZ, *President of United Farm Workers of America*
He stood in the doorway – rooted in the earth – framed by the visual symbol of the farm workers union.
Quiet and of deep moral strength, he has wrought a revolution in fair wages, health benefits, and education.

WALTER CRONKITE, *Television and Radio News Correspondent, Writer*

We share a love of the sea. Sailing on his boat, America's trusted news commentator finds a welcome respite from the split-second tensions of television journalism.

KATHARINE GRAHAM, *Publisher of* Washington Post *and* Newsweek

We spoke of our mutual admiration for the great photographer and friend of her childhood, Edward Steichen, and of the photographs I had made years ago of her distinguished parents.

ELIE WIESEL, *Nobel Laureate (Peace Prize)*

In his book-lined study, I found an erudite storyteller, a Holocaust survivor who has retained a bittersweet sense of life and placed it in the service of worldwide peace and human rights.

HENRY KISSINGER, *Nobel Laureate (Peace Prize), Former Secretary of State*
    Out of public office, but still in power; his opinions and assessments continue to influence
    world leaders.

VARTAN GREGORIAN, *President of Brown University, former Director of New York Public Library*

It was heartwarming to see the genuine pleasure, accompanied by enthusiastic hugs, with which Dr. Gregorian greeted members of his former New York Public Library staff. His spirit is still very much there.

SANDRA DAY O'CONNOR, *Supreme Court Justice*
Her serene ease and pleasant cooperation made our photographic session a delight.
Afterward, the justice was a gracious hostess at an impromptu luncheon in her chambers.

H. NORMAN SCHWARZKOPF, *U.S. Army General, Retired*
    It was easy to see why this superb military tactician merits such intense loyalty: He cares
deeply for people and is quick to show his affection and concern.

JOSEPH BAUM, *Creator of Restaurants*

Part mystic, sensitive intellectual, and innovative prophet of America's dining out, Joe Baum told me that "a restaurant is a culinary seduction — and the first to be seduced is one's self."

ANDRÉ SOLTNER, *Chef, Restaurateur*

Instead of one of Soltner's culinary masterpieces, we decided that this silver rooster, sculpted with forks and spoons, made its own droll commentary on the art of cuisine.

BOB COUSY, *Basketball Player, Coach, Commentator*

He has made the transition from his spectacular performance on the basketball court to coaching and knowledgeable commentary with the same sterling integrity and purposeful devotion.

BILLIE JEAN KING, *Tennis Player*
> Restless and energetic, she is content with neither her record-breaking Wimbledon titles nor her pioneer efforts on behalf of women in sport; she continues to be an inspirational coach and guiding spirit.

ARNOLD PALMER, *Golfer*

    The great golfer and his wife looked forward to our photographic session as to a celebration. They charmed me with their ingenuous anticipation, like children at a birthday party before the cake is served.

JOE PATERNO, *Football Coach*

He told me of his successful "grand experiment" at Penn State, begun some twenty-five years ago—to prove that a young college football player need not sacrifice academics in favor of winning.

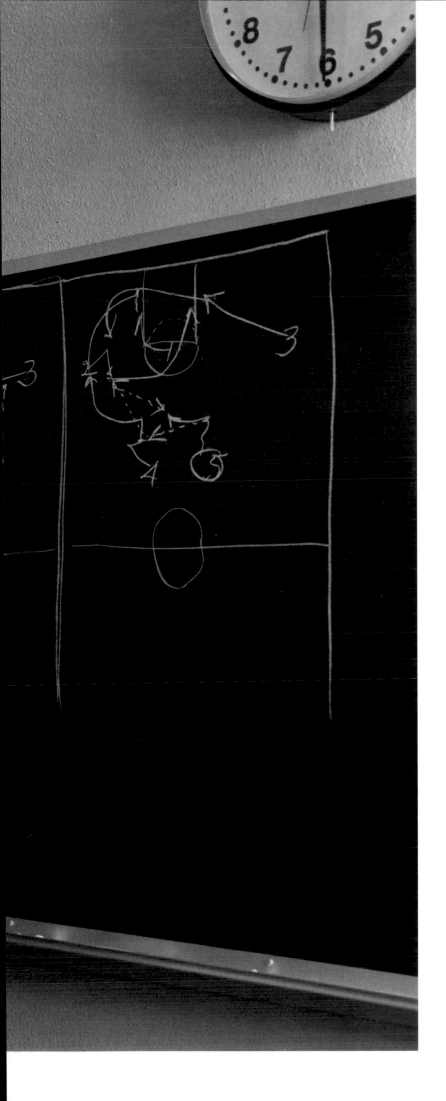

JOHN WOODEN, *Basketball Coach*

We could not walk to the UCLA John Wooden Sports Center without being surrounded by a stream of appreciative students. An inspiration on and off the basketball court, he counsels, "Do not let what you cannot do interfere with what you can do."

GORDIE HOWE, *Hockey Player*

An aristocrat of sport, this doting grandfather retains the youthful manner, boyish enthusiasm, and ease of deportment that endeared him to generations of hockey fans.

WOLFGANG PUCK, *Restaurateur, Chef*

With his daring culinary expertise, coupled with his sensitivity to ambience, he has made his restaurants contemporary watering places to the Hollywood elite.

COLLEEN DEWHURST, *Actress*

Of her upstate New York retreat, the late, beloved actress said, "This farm is my eye in the storm, my sanity, my safety, my knowledge that there is a place I do exist, that is my home."

HELEN HAYES, *Actress*

> She was animated, caring, and gracious — as much the First Lady of Thoughtfulness as of the American Theater.

JULIE HARRIS, *Actress*

Her ancient amber necklace, a talisman, evoked for her the spirit of Africa and Isak Dinesen, whose very soul Harris portrayed in her stunning one-woman show.

ANGELA LANSBURY, *Actress*

Our first photographic session was years ago, when she was a fledgling star. Now, she shared her joy
in her garden and her pride in her fine cooking, and endeared herself to me for the second time.

BILLY WILDER, *Film Director*

On the long shelf holding his leather-bound movie scripts and six Oscars spanning a fifty-year career as writer-director-producer, the Winged Victory bronze presented to him by the "divine director René Clair" was especially meaningful.

MICKEY ROONEY, *Actor*

The "King of the Movies" was the cordial king in his own home – courtly to his wife, Jan, playing the piano, surrounded by friendly dogs and a perky cockatoo, which flew from his shoulder to mine.

CHARLTON HESTON, *Actor*

At our photographic reunion after almost four decades, the youthful "Moses" and "Ben Hur" had matured into an elder statesman of film and the theater, directing, producing, and encouraging new talent.

JAMES STEWART, *Actor*

I was struck most by his quality of stillness, by his inner core of serenity. I imagine it must always have been there, and now his years have added to it a special grace.

RAY BRADBURY, *Author*

Of his prolific output of novels, short stories, and scripts, the ebullient author told me, "People love to put a label on you. I'm an idea writer, not a science fiction writer."

HELEN GURLEY BROWN, *Editor of* Cosmopolitan *Magazine, Writer*

The savvy lady who, a quarter-century ago, created "that Cosmo Girl" and launched a publishing phenomenon is still intuitively tapping into the secret desires of her readers.

CHARLES SCHULZ, *Cartoonist*

He presented me with America's favorite beagle, a tiny velvet "Snoopy," as a gift for my wife, and it remains among her favorite sentimental treasures.

AL HIRSCHFELD, *Artist*

I was happy to experience the great theater caricaturist's merry heart, and honored to be the subject of his whimsical, perceptive, nonmalicious drawing pen. "Being an artist," his friend Brendan Gill has truly said, "he has not found time to grow old."

KURT VONNEGUT, *Author*

His straightforward manner belied the wry complexity of a mind which could conceive
"random chaos beneath a seemingly logical surface."

NORMAN MAILER, *Author*

We had not seen each other in years, but the camaraderie was still there. Over a bowl of soup,
we shared jovial anecdotes and warm remembrances.

JOHN UPDIKE, *Author*

We sat together in his historic New England kitchen on a day winter suddenly became spring, and he playfully spoke of the spirits abiding in older houses and older rooms.

TOM WOLFE, *Author*

    Incisively intelligent, a Southern gentleman on the streets of New York, he says his writing combines "the emotional impact of novels, . . . the analytical insights of essays, . . . and the factual foundation of hard reporting."

Design by Carl Zahn

Photolithography and printing by Imprimerie Jean Genoud SA, Lausanne

Bound by Mayer et Soutter, Lausanne